Table of Contents:

CHAPTER 1: HOW TO BE RICH

Wealth: It's a desire shared by nearly everyone, but few actually know how to obtain it.Luck, skill, and perseverance are required to become wealthy.To become wealthy, you will first need to choose a career that will provide you with financial benefits, then you will need to prudently manage the money you earn by investing it, saving it, and cutting back on living expenses.It is not easy to become wealthy, but it is definitely doable with a little bit of perseverance and skillful decision-making.

1 of 5 methods:

Putting money into the stock market:Put your money into stocks, bonds, or other investment vehicles that will give you a return on investment (ROI) that is high enough to last through retirement.For instance, if a million dollars are invested and you receive a dependable return on investment of 7%, that equates to $70,000 annually, less inflation.

Day traders who promise to make a quick buck should not tempt you.It's basically gambling to buy and sell dozens of stocks every day.You can lose a lot of money if you make bad trades, which are ridiculously simple to do.It is not a good strategy for making money.

Learn how to invest for the long term instead.Pick good stocks and passive funds that have strong fundamentals and great leadership in industries that are poised for growth in the future.After that, let your stock rest.Nothing will be done with it.Allow it to weather the storms.Over time, you should do very well if you invest wisely.

Because they have low fees and can provide you with some relatively safe exposure to the stock market, index funds might be a good choice for you if you are just starting out with a small amount of money to invest.

2 Invest in your future:Keep investing.It would appear that fewer people are adequately saving for retirement.Some people fear that they will never be able to retire.Utilize tax-deferred retirement plans like IRAs and 401(k)s.You will be able to accelerate your retirement savings thanks to their tax treatment.

Don't rely solely on Social Security.Despite the fact that it is a safe bet that Social Security will continue to function for the next 20 or so years, some data suggest that Social Security will not be available in its current form if Congress does not radically alter the system, either by raising taxes or reducing benefits.However, it is highly likely that Congress will take action to "fix" Social Security.In any case, retirees' use of Social Security in later years was never intended to be their only option.Because of this, it is even more crucial that you invest and save money for the future.

Put money into a Roth IRA.A Roth IRA is a retirement account that allows working people to contribute $5,500 annually.After that, the money is put into investments and earns compound interest.The money you withdraw from your Roth IRA is not subject to tax if you wait until you reach retirement age because it was taxed when you first earned it.

Make a 401(k) contribution.Your employer has set up this account so that pre-tax contributions can be invested.You can get a match from your employer for all or part of your contributions.You probably won't get anywhere near "free money" in your life like this!Contribute enough to get the most out of the match.

3 Put money into real estate:A good way to build wealth is through relatively stable assets like rental properties or potential development land in an area that is always growing.There are no guarantees, as there are with any investment.However, a lot of people have had very good experiences with real estate.The value of such investments is likely to rise over time.For instance, some people believe that the value of a Manhattan apartment will almost certainly rise in any five-year period.

4 Put your time into:You might, for instance, give yourself a few hours each day to do nothing because you like having free time.However, if you were to devote those few hours to becoming wealthy, you could work toward having 20 years of leisure time (24 hours a day!)with a premature retirementWhat can you give up now to become wealthy later?"Live like no one else today so that you can live like no one else tomorrow," says investment advisor Dave Ramsey to his radio audience.

5 Don't buy things that will depreciate quickly:Spending $50,000 on a car is sometimes thought to be a waste because, regardless of how much work you put into it, it probably won't be worth half that much in five years.A brand-new automobile loses between 20 and 25 percent of its value the moment it leaves the dealership and continues to do so each year you own it.As a result, purchasing a vehicle is a significant financial decision.

6 Don't spend money on frivolous things:Making a living is already challenging.However, when the things you spend your hard-earned money on are financial black holes, it is difficult and painful.Reexamine the things you buy with your money.Determine whether they truly "are worth it."If you want to become wealthy, you probably won't want to spend that much on the following:

Tickets for lottery and casinos.Only a few are successful.The remainder of us give up.

vices, such as smoking.People who smoke a lot can only watch their money burn.

Huge markups like drinks at a club or candy at the movie theater.

Plastic surgery and tanning beds.If you want, you can get skin cancer for free outside.Also, do nose jobs and botox injections always turn out the way they were promised?Learn how to age with grace!You are not the only person aging.

Tickets for flights in first class.What will you get for that additional $1,000?A warm towel and additional leg room of 4 inches (10.2 cm)?Instead of throwing away that money, invest it.

7 Remain Rich:It's hard to become wealthy, and it's even harder to stay wealthy.The market will always have an impact on your wealth, and the market has its ups and downs.When the market goes down, you'll quickly find yourself back where you started if you get too comfortable during good times.Don't spend more money if you get a raise, promotion, or percentage point increase in ROI.Keep it for times when business is slow and your return on investment drops by two percentage points.

5th Method 2:

Enriching Your Life with a Career 1 Perform Well in School:Some successful people go to college after high school, whether it's a four-year institution or a vocational school.Employers can only judge you by your educational background in the beginning stages of your career.Salary increases typically follow higher grades.

2 Pick the right occupation:Take a look at salary surveys to learn about the median annual earnings for various occupations.If you choose a career in finance over teaching, your chances of becoming wealthy are lower.The following are some of America's highest-paying jobs:

surgeons and doctors.Anesthesiologists earn more than $200,000 annually.

Petroleum specialists.Engineers who work for oil and gas companies can earn a lot of money.They typically earn more than $135,000 annually.

Attorneys.If you're willing to put in the effort, law school can pay well over $130,000 per year, making it a lucrative career choice.

Software engineers and managers in IT.If you're good at programming and know your way around computers, this is a very well-paying job.IT managers typically earn $125,000 annually.

3 Select the appropriate location:Go to where there are good jobs.For instance, if you want to work in finance, big cities offer more opportunities than rural, sparsely populated areas.If you want to start a business, you should probably think about moving to Silicon

Valley.Go to Los Angeles or New York City if you want to break into the entertainment business big time.

4 Start at the bottom and work your way up:Play the game of numbers.Put yourself through a lot of interviews and apply to a lot of places.Stay with your current job to gain the experience you need to advance.

5 Change employers and jobs:Consider looking for a new job once you've gained some experience.You can experience different corporate cultures and increase your pay by changing your environment.Do this multiple times without hesitation.If your current employer knows you're considering leaving, they might also give you a raise or other benefits if they think you're a valuable employee.

5. Method 3:

1 Way to Cut Costs of Living Try extreme couponing:When you are able to get paid to bring home things that you frequently use, it is one of the best feelings in the world.Couponing can actually pay you if done correctly.At best, you'll be able to put a few extra dollars away for emergencies.At best, you'll get a lot of free stuff and increase your wealth.

2 Buy a lot:Although it is not the simplest method of shopping, it is typically the most effective.If you can get a loan or sign up for a Costco membership, it might make sense financially.Brand-name products can sometimes be purchased at significant discounts.

Buy four pre-cooked chickens at Costco when they go on sale at the end of the day if you're hungry and like chicken.You can get at least ten hearty meals for about $1 each when they drop from $5 each to $2.50 each on occasion!Any chickens you don't eat right away put in the freezer.

3. Learn how to can food:In the United States, up to 40% of food is wasted before it is used.It is possible to can succulent peaches, blueberries, and even meats and store them for later consumption.Make smart choices about the food you buy.Consume it in fact.Money is lost when food is wasted.

4 Cut down on your utility costs:If you let them, utilities like gas and electricity can have a significant impact on your monthly budget.Don't, then.Think strategically about how to keep your house warm in the winter and cool in the summer.If you want to convert the sun's natural energy into electricity, you might even want to think about building or investing in solar panels.Keep your utility costs low, and you'll start to save money.

5 Get an energy audit of your home:You will be able to determine the amount of money that is being lost from your home due to unused energy thanks to this.

If you're the kind of person who works hard, you can do your own energy audit, but you should hire a professional to do it for you.It should cost between $300 and $500, which isn't cheap. However, if you decide to re-insulate the house, it could help you save much more over time.

6 Try foraging or hunting for food:If you already have the necessary equipment and permits, this is a cost-effective method of obtaining your own food.It is fairly simple to forage for food if you are ethically opposed to the killing of animals, depending on where you live.Just

be sure to only forage for food of known origin and properties.Poisoning or getting sick is never fun.

Choose edible flowers, pick wild mushrooms, or forage for food in the fall. Start guerrilla gardening or build your own greenhouse. Go deer, duck, or turkey hunting. Go fishing or fly fishing.

4 Saving Money

1: Prioritize yourself.Put money aside in an account you don't touch before you spend your paycheck on a new pair of shoes or a golf club you don't need.Watch as your account grows by doing this each time you get paid.

2 Create a spending plan and stick to it.Create a monthly budget that covers all of your essential costs and includes some money for "fun."A good way to prepare for your efforts to become wealthy is to stick to your budget and save at least some money each month.

3 Upgrade your vehicle and home.Could you live in an apartment rather than a house or with roommates rather than in your own home?Is it possible to buy a used car rather than a brand-new one and use it less frequently?All of these methods can help you save a lot of money each month.

4 Reduce costs.Reevaluate everything by taking a look at the frivolous ways you spend money.Take, for instance, not going to Starbucks each morning.Every morning, you spend $4 on designer coffee, which equates to $28 per week or $1,460 over a year!

5 Keep track of your spending.It is essential to keep track of your expenses if you want to cut costs more effectively.Choose one of the

many available applications for tracking expenses, such as Money Lover or Mint, and keep track of each and every dollar that enters and exits your wallet.You should be able to determine where the majority of your money goes and what you can do about it after about three months.

6 Use your refund from taxes wisely.The average tax refund in the United States was $2,733 in 2007.That is a substantial sum!Can you put that money toward paying off debts or starting an emergency fund instead of spending it on something that will soon lose half its value?It could be worth ten times as much in the same amount of time if you invest nearly $3,000.

7 Disband using your credit card.Did you know that when making purchases, people who use credit cards spend more money than those who use cash?This is because it hurts to part with money.Using a credit card doesn't hurt nearly as much.Divorce your credit card if you can and see how it feels to pay cash.Most likely, you will save a lot of money.

Do things to cut costs if you do have a credit card.Make an effort to pay off the entire balance each month on time.As a result, you get credit without interest.To avoid paying a late fee, at the very least, make the minimum monthly payment before the due date.

5th approach:

Refinance your home mortgage to get rid of your mortgage.Refinance to a 15-year loan instead of a 30-year loan or a lower rate.Even though you will pay a few hundred dollars more each month, you will save much more in total interest.

For instance, if you take out a 30-year loan for $200,000 and make additional interest payments of $186,500, you will end up paying a total of $386,500 over the course of 30 years.On the other hand, if you are willing to pay a few extra hundred dollars per month—for instance, $350—by refinancing to a 15-year loan with a lower interest rate, you can pay off your mortgage in just 15 years, and the best part is that you will save a whopping $123,700 on interest.That is cash in your account.Discuss your options with a loan officer.You are not alone if you wish you had a little more money in your pocket.Fortunately, you can earn money in a number of different ways.It's simple and quick to make money doing odd jobs.In a similar vein, selling things you make or resell can help you make more money.Another way to make money online is to write a blog, work as a freelancer, or take surveys online.

Things You Need to Know Earn money while you're not working.For instance, charge people who need landscaping, babysitting, or tutoring.

CHAPTER 2 :HOW TO MAKE MONEY

The internet is an excellent source of quick cash.Fill out paid online surveys or resell items like thrifted clothes.

Or, make something valuable and sell it for a lot of money.Take up flipping houses or restoring old furniture.

method 1:Odd Jobs

1: Start a pet-sitting or dog-walking business.Pet care is a great way to get some exercise and earn extra cash without breaking the bank.Use a personal website or your local classifieds to promote your services online.You can also sign up for an account with a service like Rover.

Before you hire someone, make sure you tell them about the services you offer.You could, for instance, specify that you will walk dogs, give all pets food and water, and play with them.You could, however, state that you will not administer medication.

2 If you are good with children, you could babysit for extra money.Talk to people you know to see if they need a babysitter, and frequently advertise your availability on social media.To get more customers, you could also sign up for an account on a website like Care.com.

If you want to babysit, getting certified in CPR is a good idea because it makes you more marketable to clients and keeps the kids safer.Image: Make Money Step 33 If you are very knowledgeable about a subject, you could become a tutor.Find out how much tutors in your area earn online.Next, select a subject that you are well-versed in and a grade level at which you can teach with ease.Post flyers, advertise yourself as a tutor online, and talk to people you know.

You could, for instance, offer to tutor students in algebra or trigonometry if you have a degree in math.Students could benefit from your assistance with writing or grammar if you have an English degree.

4 Provide services for landscaping.Distribute flyers and business cards to promote your services as a local landscaper.Be specific about the tasks you can do, such as manicure plants, clear brush, and

mow lawns.Hedges and flower beds can be planted if you are good at gardening.

Don't provide any services that you haven't done before.You could lose a lot of business if you disappoint a customer.

Tip:Ask satisfied customers to recommend your company to others.Often, the best way to acquire new customers is through word of mouth.

5 Complete elderly-related chores or errands.Buying groceries, cleaning, maintaining their homes, and paying their bills are all tasks that older people frequently require assistance with.To find customers, inquire with your neighborhood church or community center to see if anyone requires assistance.You could also advertise in the local classifieds or inquire with people you know to see if they know of anyone in need of assistance.

You could, for instance, devote a few hours each week to paying bills, cleaning a client's home, and going grocery shopping for them.

6 For extra cash, look online for odd jobs.Every day, look for work on sites like Craigslist, Fiverr, and Zaarly.You might be able to help people with errands, distribute flyers for upcoming events, clean up trash, or take care of minor home repairs.

Always respond with caution to online advertisements.It's probably a scam if a show sounds too good to be true.

Variation:You can also look for tasks that pay you to do using apps.You can connect with people who are looking for someone to do odd jobs for them by using apps like GigWalk and Task Rabbit, for instance.

method 2:Earning Money Online

Start a blog or website.Start a website or blog about what you love, and then post something new every day.Try to provide something useful to your readers so that they keep coming back.Put ads on your website, include paid content, or sell subscriptions that give you access to more content to make money.

Making money from a website or blog can take some time, and there is a lot of competition.However, making money this way is doable.

Variation:You might try selling affiliate products to make extra money, depending on the subject of your blog or website.This entails linking to products on Amazon or other retailers' websites.You will make money if your readers click on the items and buy them.

2: Work as a freelancer in a field in which you are an expert.You can sell your services directly to customers who require them if you have a skill that is in high demand.On a personal website, advertise your services and look for freelancing work on platforms like Upwork, Freelancer, and Fivrr.Also, give out business cards and ask satisfied customers to tell their friends about your work.As a freelancer, there are a few ways to make money:

Perform coding or programming.

Create websites.

Design graphics.

Write.

Proofread or edit.

If you have experience, work as a consultant.

3 Take part in online surveys to win more money or gift cards.Even though online surveys don't pay much, they can help you make money while you're not working.Rewards in cash could be yours if you complete a lot of surveys.However, a legitimate website will not charge you to sign up, so don't pay to join a survey company.Try out these survey websites:

Junkie User Testing Mind Field Online Tip: Global Test Market SurveyYou might want to set up a separate email account just for taking online surveys because once you start, you'll probably get a lot of marketing emails.

Method 3:Reselling

 1: Sell things you no longer need.It's possible that someone else will pay you a few dollars for your old tools, clothes, DVDs, CDs, video games, records, books, and household items.You can sell your items at a yard sale, at a local resale shop, or online.

Frequently, resale shops concentrate on a single item, such as video games, clothing, or books.Find a store in your area by searching online.

Try Ebay or Amazon if you want to sell your goods online.You can also sell your items locally by using Craigslist or your neighborhood classifieds.

2 Use online auctions to repurpose clothes and accessories from yard sales or thrift stores.Try to find clothes and accessories that are still in good shape, especially those from well-known brands.Utilize online marketplaces like Ebay, Etsy, and Depop to advertise your products for sale.They should be priced so that you can sell them for a profit even after you pay for shipping.

Be patient because selling your products might take some time.

Look up the items you want to resell to get an idea of how much they sell for when you first start.Then, add the estimated costs of shipping, which can be found on the website of your local postal service.This ensures that you don't accidentally overpay for the items.

It's best to stick with things you already know about.For instance, select brands that are simple to recognize or shop at stores you are familiar with.In a similar vein, you might concentrate on goods in which you have some expertise, such as vintage video games or designer handbags.

Variation:You could also resell items on clearance from well-known retailers.You might be able to resell these new items online for a profit if you combine sale prices with coupons or store loyalty points.

3 Look for used books that are cheap enough to sell online.You can scan the barcodes on books by downloading an app that can read ISBN numbers.This will show you the current price of the book on Amazon, allowing you to determine whether it is worth trying to resell it.The next step is to search garage sales, thrift shops, and used book stores for high-value books.Utilize sites like Amazon and Ebay to advertise the books for sale online.

Perseverance is essential because you might have to scan a lot of books before you find one that is worth reselling.

As you do this, it's best to keep a low profile.

4 If you have experience fixing up homes, try flipping them.If you've ever watched popular shows about home improvement, you might be aware that flipping houses entails purchasing a less expensive property that requires repairs before preparing it for resale.You will need financing, either from a partner or a bank, to get started.You can then purchase a property at a price lower than its market value.You might be able to sell the property for a profit after you renovate it.

Although it may appear glamorous on television, flipping houses is actually extremely difficult and dirty work.It's probably not a good idea to try flipping houses if you don't know how to fix things in homes.

method 4:Making Products

1: Sell jewelry and handmade crafts at local events or through an online store.Make products that you can sell with your crafting skills.After that, create an online store using a platform like Etsy.Set up a booth to sell your products at local gatherings, festivals, and events to boost sales.

Before signing up for a booth, make sure you know how much it will cost because some events require vendors to pay a fee to sell their products.

Tip:Include the cost of the materials in your product pricing.Additionally, keep track of how long you spend working on your items to approximate your hourly earnings.

2 Work for yourself as a photographer and sell your work online.Do photography sessions or take photos of events like parties and weddings if you have a high-quality DSLR camera.Take stock photos to sell online on sites like iStock Photo, Shutterstock, or Alamy, or create fine art photos that people might want to hang on their walls.

You will need to create a portfolio of your work in order to get a job as a photographer.Before charging people for these photos, you might offer to volunteer your services at a few events for free.

Before posting any artistic or stock photos of people for sale, make sure you get their signed consent form.

3 Refinish old furniture that you find at garage sales, thrift stores, or online ads.Sand the furniture to remove some of the old stain or paint and smooth out the surfaces.Use paint thinner or lacquer to remove the stain if you want to refinish it.

CHAPTER 3:HOW TO SAVE MONEYMONEY

 Put some of your earnings into a retirement or savings account.Pay off any existing debt and avoid accumulating new debt.Set a time frame for your savings goals that is attainable.Keep track of all your expenses and make a budget.If you are familiar with the ins and outs of taking risks, you should not invest in the stock market.Only spend money on what is absolutely necessary, and when you can, look for less expensive options for things like housing, food, transportation, and energy use.Make savings for an emergency fund.Rarely spend money on frivolous pursuits.

Part 1 of Three:

Paying yourself first is a responsible way to save money.The simplest way to save money rather than spend it is to ensure that you never have the opportunity to do so.When you arrange for a portion of each paycheck to be deposited directly into a savings or retirement account, the process of deciding how much money to save and how much to keep for yourself each month is less stressful and more time-consuming. In other words, you save automatically, and the money you keep each month is yours to spend as you please.Putting even a small portion of each paycheck into savings can add up over time, especially when interest is taken into account. To get the most out of it, start as soon as you can.

Talk to your employer's payroll staff or, if your employer uses one, your third-party payroll service to set up an automatic deposit.You should generally be able to set up a direct deposit program without any problems if you are able to provide account information for a savings account that is distinct from your standard checking account.

If you can't set up an automatic deposit for each paycheck (for example, if you make your living as a freelancer or get most of your pay in cash), set a specific amount of cash to manually deposit into a savings account each month and stick to it.

2 Avoid accruing additional debt.It is almost impossible to avoid some debt.For instance, only the extremely wealthy have enough money to purchase a home in one lump sum, but millions of people

are able to do so by taking out loans and gradually repaying them.However, generally speaking, avoid debt whenever possible.In the long run, it is always cheaper to pay a sum of money up front than to pay off a similar loan while interest builds up over time.

Try to put as much money down as you can if you have to take out a loan.You'll pay off your loan faster and pay less in interest if you can cover more of the purchase cost up front.

Although each person's financial situation is unique, the majority of banks advise keeping debt payments to less than 20% of pretax income, which is considered healthy.A "upper limit" for debt of a reasonable amount is thought to be 36 percent.

3 Set attainable savings objectives.When you are aware that you have something to save for, saving becomes much simpler.To motivate yourself to make the difficult financial decisions necessary to save responsibly, set savings goals that are within your reach.It may take years or decades to achieve serious goals like buying a house or retiring.In these instances, regular progress monitoring is essential.You can only gain an understanding of how far you have come and how far you still have to go by taking a step back and looking at the big picture.

It takes a very long time to achieve big goals like retirement.Financial markets are likely to change over time in order to achieve these objectives.Before establishing your objective, you might need to conduct some research into the market's anticipated future state.For instance, according to the majority of financial commentators, if you are in your prime earning years, you will need between 60 and 85 percent of your current annual income each year to maintain your current lifestyle once you retire.

4 Set a timetable for your objectives.A great way to motivate yourself is to set ambitious but manageable deadlines for achieving your objectives.Let's say, for instance, that you decided you wanted to be in possession of a home in two years.In this scenario, you would need to look into the average price of a home in the area you want to live in and start saving for the down payment on your new home (down payments typically need to be at least 20% of the purchase price).

So, in our example, if the houses in the area you're interested in are each around $300,000, you'll need at least $300,000 x 20% = $60,000 in two years.This might or might not be possible for you, depending on your income.

Particularly crucial for essential short-term objectives is the establishment of time frames.For instance, if the transmission in your car needs to be replaced but you can't afford to buy a new one, you should start saving as soon as possible to make sure you won't be stuck without a way to get to work.You can achieve this objective with an ambitious but manageable time frame.

5 Follow a budget.It's easy to set ambitious savings goals, but if you can't keep track of your expenses, it will be hard to achieve them.Try budgeting your monthly income each month to keep your financial progress on track.If you divide each paycheck according to your budget as soon as you receive it, allocating a predetermined portion of your income to all of your major expenses can help ensure that you do not waste money.

For instance, we could budget as follows for a monthly income of $3,000.

Housing/utilities:Student loans for $1,000:$300

Food:Internet, $500:$70 for gas:$150 saved:$500

Misc.:luxuries for $200:$280 6 Keep track of your expenses.If you want to save money, you need to stick to a strict budget. However, if you don't keep track of your expenses, it may be difficult to achieve your objectives.You can identify "problem" areas and adjust your spending habits to fit your budget by keeping a running tally of how much you spend on various expenses each month.However, meticulous attention to detail can be required when tracking expenses.While major expenses like housing and debt repayment should be tracked by everyone, the amount of attention you give to minor expenses typically increases with the severity of your financial situation.

Having a small notebook with you at all times can be useful.Make it a habit to keep track of all expenses and keep receipts, especially for major purchases.For long-term records, enter your expenses whenever possible in a larger notebook or a spreadsheet program.

Keep in mind that you can now download a variety of apps to your phone to help you keep track of your expenses—some of which are free.

Don't be afraid to keep every receipt if you have serious spending issues.Sort your receipts into categories at the end of the month, and then add them up.You might be surprised by how much money you spend on things that aren't really necessary.

7 Verify each payment amount twice.When you make a purchase in person, always ask for the receipt, and whenever you buy something online, always print a copy.Check to see if you're not being overcharged or charged for things you don't want;You won't believe how frequently that occurs.

Imagine you and your friends are at a bar and one of them orders margaritas for the group;ensure that they do not end up on your card.One way to run into financial trouble, potentially one that is very, very deep, is to rely on favors like this one to be returned later.

Avoid splitting the cost out of convenience.You shouldn't be responsible for paying half of the bill if your meal costs displaystyle 1/31/3 more than that of your friends.

To assist you in accurately calculating tips, think about downloading a smartphone app.

8 Begin saving as soon as you can.Savings account deposits typically earn interest at a predetermined percentage rate.The amount of interest you earn from your savings account grows over time.Therefore, it is in your best interest to begin saving as soon as possible.Do so, even if you can only make a small monthly contribution to your savings when you are in your twenties.Small amounts of cash kept in accounts that pay interest for a long time can eventually grow to several times their original value.

Take, for instance, the scenario in which you work a low-paying job in your twenties and eventually save $10,000, which you then put into a high-yield account with an annual interest rate of 4%.This will pay you about $2,166.53 over five years.However, you would have earned approximately $500 more at the same time if you had saved this money one year earlier, which is a modest but not insignificant bonus.

9 Think about putting money into a retirement account.Retirement can seem so far away when you're young, energised, and healthy that it almost seems pointless to even consider it.It might be all you think about when you get older and start to lose steam.Once you have established a stable career, you will need to start saving for retirement, even if you are one of the fortunate few who stand to inherit significant wealth. The earlier you start, the better.Even though almost everyone's situation is unique, it's wise to anticipate having 60-85% of your annual income available for each year that you are retired to maintain your current standard of living.

If you haven't already, discuss the possibility of making 401(k) contributions with your employer.Saving money is simple with these retirement accounts because you can set a predetermined amount to be deposited into the account each paycheck.In addition, the money you put into a 401(k) may not be taxed in the same way as the rest of your paycheck.Lastly, many companies provide 401(k) services with proportional matching programs, in which they will match a predetermined percentage of each payment.

The maximum amount you can contribute to a 401(k) each year as of 2014 is $17,500.

10 Be cautious when investing in the stock market.Investing in the stock market can be a lucrative but risky way to make extra money if you've been saving responsibly and have some spare cash.It is essential to comprehend that any money invested in the stock market could potentially be permanently lost, particularly if you do

not know what you are doing. As a result, you should not use this strategy for long-term savings.Instead, view the stock market as an opportunity to basically take calculated risks with money you can afford to lose.To save responsibly for retirement, most people don't even need to invest in the stock market.

See How to Invest in the Stock Market for additional guidance on smart stock investment decisions.

11 Don't get down on yourself.It's easy to lose your courage when you can't save money.Your circumstance may appear hopeless; it may appear nearly impossible to save the money required to achieve your long-term objectives.However, it is always possible to begin saving money, regardless of how little you start with.The sooner you begin, the sooner you can achieve financial independence.

Talk to a financial counseling service if your financial situation is making you feel down.These organizations, which frequently provide their services at no cost or at very low costs, are there to assist you in starting to save money so that you can achieve your financial objectives.A great place to start is the non-profit National Foundation for Credit Counseling (NFCC).

2

First, cut back on luxuries from your budget.It would be prudent to begin here if you are having trouble saving money.Many of the expenses we take for granted are not even close to being necessary.Because it won't have a significant impact on your quality of life or your ability to perform your work, cutting back on luxury expenses is a great first step toward improving your financial situation.You might be surprised at how simple it is to live without a cable TV subscription and a gas-guzzling car once you get rid of both of these things from your life.Here are a few easy ways to cut back on spending on luxury items:

Unsubscribe from optional internet or television bundles.

Switch your phone's service plan to one that costs less.

Replace a costly vehicle with one that uses less gas and costs less to maintain.

Sell any unused electronic devices.

Shop at thrift stores for clothes and home goods.

2 Look for cheaper housing.The majority of people's budgets are dominated by housing-related expenses.Saving money for housing can therefore free up a significant portion of your income for other essential activities like retirement savings.If you're having trouble keeping your finances in check, you should seriously reevaluate your housing situation, even though doing so is not always simple.

If you're renting, you might try negotiating a lower rent with your landlord.If you have a good relationship with your landlord, you might be able to get a better deal because most landlords want to avoid the risk of looking for new tenants.You might be able to get a lower rent by doing work that pays less, like gardening or housekeeping.

Talk to your lender about refinancing your loan if you are paying a mortgage.If you are in good standing, you might be able to get a better deal by negotiating.Try to keep the repayment schedule as short as possible when refinancing.

You might also want to think about moving entirely to a housing market where prices are lower.A recent study found that Detroit, Michigan, has the most affordable housing markets in the United States;Michigan county of Lake;Ohio's Cleveland;Florida's Palm Bay;and Ohio's Toledo.

3 Get cheap food.A lot of people spend more on food than they need to.When you're enjoying a gourmet meal at your favorite restaurant, it's easy to forget to be thrifty. However, if expenses related to food are allowed to spiral out of control, they can quickly mount up.In general, purchasing large quantities of food is less expensive in the long run than purchasing smaller quantities; if your food costs are high, you might want to sign up for a membership at a warehouse retailer like Costco.The most expensive way to eat out is to try to eat in rather than go out, as buying individual meals at restaurants is the most expensive option.

Choose healthy, inexpensive foods.Try browsing the fresh food and produce sections of your neighborhood grocery store rather than purchasing prepared or processed foods.How inexpensive it is to eat well may surprise you!Brown rice, for instance, is a filling and nutritious food that can be purchased in large sacks weighing twenty pounds for less than a dollar per pound.

Make use of special offers.At the checkout counter, many grocery stores, particularly large chains, offer coupons and discounts.These should not be wasted!

Stop going out to eat frequently.Cooking a meal at home typically costs less than ordering a comparable dish from a restaurant.Cooking on a regular basis teaches you a useful skill that you can use to satisfy your family, entertain friends, and even attract romantic interest.

If your situation is serious, don't be afraid to use free food resources in your area.Those in need can get free meals from shelters, food banks, and soup kitchens.For more information if you require assistance, contact your local Department of Social Services.

4 Cut back on your energy use.The majority of people simply accept the monthly utility bill price.In fact, with just a few easy steps, you can significantly reduce your energy use and, as a result, your monthly bill.If you want to save money, there's practically no reason not to use these easy tricks.Best of all, reducing your energy consumption also reduces your indirect emissions of pollution, minimizing your impact on the global environment.

When you are not present, turn off the lights.When you leave the house or room, turn off the lights because there is no need to keep them on.If you're having trouble remembering, you could try leaving a sticky note by the door.

When not absolutely necessary, turn off the air conditioning and heating.Open your windows or use a small personal fan to keep cool.Wear multiple layers of clothing, use a blanket, or use a space heater to stay warm.

Put money into good insulation.By preventing the warm or cool interior air from escaping, replacing old, leaky insulation in your walls with high-efficiency modern insulation can save you money in the long run if you can afford to pay for a significant home improvement project.

Put money into solar panels if you can.Solar panels are the way to go as a serious investment in your own future and the future of the planet.Despite the high initial costs, solar technology is becoming more and more affordable every year.

5 Take less expensive means of transportation.Maintaining and driving a car can consume a significant portion of your income.Fuel can set you back hundreds of dollars a month, depending on how much you drive.In addition, you'll have to pay for licensing and upkeep for your car.Utilize a less expensive or free alternative method rather than driving.This will not only help you save money, but it could also give you more time to exercise and lessen the stress of your daily commute.

Find options for public transportation in your area.Depending on where you live, you might be able to take public transportation at a low cost.In most large cities, you can use bus or train systems, while in mid-sized towns, you can use metro, subway, or streetcar lines to get in and out of the city.

Think about biking or walking to work.If you live close enough to your job to be able to do this, both are great ways to get to work for free while getting some exercise and fresh air.

You can save time and money by booking your train and flight tickets in advance online.For those who book early, "Early bird" deals frequently exist.

Carpooling is an option to consider if driving is not an option.You can share the costs of fuel and upkeep with the other carpool members by doing this.Additionally, you'll have someone to talk to on the way to work.

6 Have fun without breaking the bank.While cutting back on frivolous luxuries can mean cutting back on personal expenses, saving money does not necessarily mean giving up having fun.You can find the right balance between having fun and taking care of your responsibilities by switching your leisure activities and habits to ones that are less expensive.If you're creative, you might be surprised at how much fun you can have for a few dollars!

Keep up with community activities.Nowadays, most cities and towns have online events calendars that list upcoming events in the area.Most of the time, events put on by community associations or the local government are cheap or even free.For instance, free art exhibitions, movie screenings in a nearby park, and community rallies that rely on donations are frequently available in medium-sized towns.

Read.Books are less expensive than movies and video games, especially when purchased used.Good books can be absolutely captivating because they let you see life through the eyes of interesting characters and teach you things you might not have known otherwise.

Take advantage of free outings with friends.There are a plethora of inexpensive activities you and your friends can participate in.Try going on a hike, playing a board game, going to a cheap second-run theater to see an old movie, exploring a part of town you haven't been to before, or playing sports.

7 Stay away from costly addictions.Your efforts to save money can be seriously hindered by certain bad habits.In the worst-case scenario, these behaviors may develop into severe addictions that are nearly

impossible to break without assistance.Worse still, many of these addictions have the potential to be extremely harmful to your health over time.By avoiding these addictions in the first place, you will not only spare your body but also your wallet the trouble of engaging in them.

Avoid smoking.The negative effects of smoking are well-known today.Smoking is known to cause lung cancer, heart disease, stroke, and a number of other serious illnesses.In addition, cigarettes cost upwards of $14 per pack, depending on where you live.

Don't drink too much.Even though having a few drinks with friends won't hurt you, drinking a lot of alcohol on a regular basis can lead to serious long-term issues like liver disease, impaired mental function, weight gain, delirium, and even death.Additionally, maintaining an alcohol addiction can be extremely costly.

Do not engage in drug abuse.Heroin, cocaine, and methamphetamine are among the most addictive drugs on the market. In addition to being significantly more expensive than alcohol and tobacco, these substances can have a variety of seriously harmful (even fatal) effects on your health.Country singer Waylon Jennings, for instance, is said to have once spent more than $1,500 per day on cocaine.

3:

Spending Sensibly 1: Prioritize spending on absolutely necessary items.There are some things that you absolutely, positively cannot live without when it comes to spending money.When it comes to spending your money, the things you need most are food, water, a place to live, and clothing.It goes without saying that achieving the rest of your financial goals will be extremely difficult if you become homeless or starve, so you should make sure you have enough money to cover these basic necessities first.

However, just because things like shelter, water, and food are important doesn't mean you have to spend a lot of money on them.For instance, cutting back on how often you eat out is a simple way to drastically cut back on food costs.Moving to a location with low rent or home prices is another great way to save money on housing.

Housing costs can eat up a lot of your income, depending on where you live.The majority of experts generally advise against accepting any housing arrangement that will exceed one-third of your income.

2 Put money away for an emergency fund.Start contributing to an emergency fund right away if you don't already have one with enough money to cover your expenses in the event of a sudden loss of income.In the event that you lose your job, having a reasonable amount of money in a safe savings account gives you the freedom to comfortably manage your finances.After you have paid for the essentials, you should put a portion of your income toward building up this savings account until you have enough money saved to cover your living costs for three to six months.

Keep in mind that living costs can fluctuate according to the local economic climate.Even though you could live on $1,500 for a few months in Detroit or Phoenix, it might not even cover one month's rent in a cheap apartment in New York City.Naturally, you'll need a larger emergency fund if you live in a pricey area.

Having an emergency fund can not only give you the assurance that you will be fine in the event of career difficulties, but it can also help you save money in the long run.If you lose your job and don't have money saved up for an emergency, you might have to take the first job you get, even if it doesn't pay much.On the other hand, if you can get by for a while without working, you can afford to be much more selective and possibly find a job with better pay.

3 Get rid of your debt.Debt can seriously hinder your efforts to save money if left unchecked.If you only make the minimum payments on your debt, you will pay much more over the loan's life than if you had paid it off sooner.By devoting a significant portion of your income to debt repayment, you can pay off your debt as quickly as possible and save money in the long run.Paying off your loans with the highest interest first is usually the best use of your money.

You will be able to safely devote almost all of your extra income to paying off your debt once you have covered your essentials and established an emergency fund of a manageable size.On the other hand, if you don't have an emergency fund, you might have to divide up your extra income so that you use some of it each month to pay off your debt and put some of it in your emergency fund.

Consider combining your debts if you have multiple sources of debt that are becoming too much for you to handle.You might be able to consolidate all of your debts into one low-interest loan.However, it's important to keep in mind that these consolidated loans may have longer repayment terms than your initial debt.

You could also try directly negotiating a lower interest rate with your lender.Your lender may agree to a lower interest rate in order to let you pay off the loan because it is not in their best interest for you to file for bankruptcy.

4 Next, put money away.You should probably start putting the extra money in a savings account as soon as you have established an emergency fund and paid off all (or nearly all) of your debt.The money you save in this way is not the same as your emergency fund. While you should only use your emergency fund when absolutely necessary, your normal savings can be used for big, important purchases like car repairs.However, you should generally avoid spending your savings in order to increase your total savings over time.Start saving 10% to 15% of your monthly income in your 20s if you can; the majority of experts agree that this is a healthy goal.

It can be tempting to buy something on the spot when you get paid.Put your savings in an account as soon as you get paid to avoid this.For instance, if you are trying to save 10% of your income and receive a paycheck for $710.68, deposit 10% immediately, or $71.07, by moving the decimal point one space to the left.You might be able to save a lot of money over time and avoid spending money you don't need.

Automating as much of the saving process as you can so that you don't even have the tempting money at first is an even better idea.For instance, inquire about setting up an automatic deposit system with your bank or a third-party app with your employer.Using this method, you can effortlessly transfer a predetermined amount or percentage of each paycheck to a savings or checking account.

5 Invest wisely in non-essentials.You should think about making certain non-essential investments that can enhance your productivity,

earning potential, and quality of life in the long run if, after contributing a healthy portion of your income to your savings each month, you have additional funds.Even though these kinds of purchases aren't as important as things like food, water, and housing, they are smart long-term decisions that can save you money in the long run.

For instance, purchasing an ergonomic chair to sit in while working is not absolutely necessary, but it is a smart long-term decision because it enables you to complete more work while reducing back pain—which, coincidentally, can be costly to treat if it becomes serious.The replacement of your home's old, troublesome water heater is another example.When you buy a new one, you won't have to spend money on repairs when the old one breaks, saving money in the long run. The old one may have been sufficient in the short term.

Purchases that make it easier for you to work, like posture-improving gel inserts for your shoes, tools that help you work more effectively, like a phone headset if you're in a job that uses your hands, and purchases that allow you to get to work for less money, like monthly or annual public transit passes, are additional examples.

6 Purchase luxuries last.Living a spartan lifestyle is not the only way to save money.It's okay to spend a little money on yourself after paying off your debt, starting an emergency fund, and making smart purchases that pay off in the long run.Don't be afraid to celebrate getting your finances in order with a reasonable luxury purchase; healthy, responsible spending is one way to stay sane while working hard.

Anything that isn't a necessary good or service and doesn't help you in the long run is considered a luxury.Trips to expensive restaurants, vacations, brand-new automobiles, cable television, expensive gadgets, and many other things fall into this broad category.